Original title:
The Blooming Mind

Copyright © 2025 Creative Arts Management OÜ
All rights reserved.

Author: Adrian Caldwell
ISBN HARDBACK: 978-1-80566-749-0
ISBN PAPERBACK: 978-1-80566-819-0

Melodies of the Mind Garden

In the garden, thoughts dance bright,
Singing tunes both day and night.
A gopher plays the ukulele,
While daisies wiggle, quite so fray.

Silly whispers float in air,
Jokes exchanged with frizzy hair.
A squirrel juggles acorns high,
As butterflies laugh, oh my, oh my!

Spiritual Seedlings

Tiny sprouts with giggles sprout,
In sacred soil, they dance about.
Roots of laughter twist and twine,
Spreading joy, oh how divine.

They plot with worms for muddy pranks,
Designing ships from fallen planks.
Their dreams sprout wings to soar so high,
Catching clouds that pass on by.

Radiance of the Heart

A sunbeam wears a funny hat,
Tickling flowers, imagine that!
Honey bees join in the game,
Buzzing laughter lifts the same.

Glowing hearts in merry rows,
Moonlit dances, giggles flows.
Each twinkle sparkles with delight,
Creating magic, day and night.

Vibrant Threads of Perception

Colors spin in wild delight,
Weaving dreams both bold and bright.
A tapestry of silly sights,
Where laughter piques and joy ignites.

Threads like ribbons, twist and twirl,
Ticklish moments start to swirl.
Each mindset wears a vibrant hue,
In this wacky world, we're brand new!

Amethyst Insights

In a world where thoughts pirouette,
Ideas bloom like a funky pet.
Bubble gum dreams, they dance and sing,
Turning dull moments to a vibrant fling.

Jellybean wishes flop and glide,
In the sweet playground where thoughts collide.
Tickle your brain, let laughter flow,
With amethyst sparks, let the silliness grow.

Harmonies of the Heart

There's a beat in every silly thought,
Juggling emotions that can't be bought.
Wobble with joy, sway with delight,
As feelings bloom in silly flight.

Banana peels underfoot, oh dear!
Yet laughter chimes like a bell so clear.
Dance in the chaos, sing through the strife,
This wacky rhythm is the spark of life!

Springs of Awareness

Bouncing ideas like springs in the air,
Each quirky notion spins without care.
Laughter erupts, a funny surprise,
As silly wisdom opens our eyes.

Worms in suits with top hats on high,
Debate the meaning of blueberry pie.
In the garden of thoughts, hilarity swells,
Where even the flowers giggle and yell.

A Symphony of Color

Colors collide in a wobbly dance,
Daffodil dreams take a chance.
A purple polka dot with a green mustache,
Brings the giggles in a splendid flash.

Canvas of laughter, hues far and wide,
Doodles that bounce, what a silly ride!
Every brushstroke is a ticklish tease,
As the symphony plays with joyful ease.

Radiant Reveries

Thoughts like flowers dance and sway,
In a garden where silliness plays.
Bees in shades of purple hats,
Buzz around like cheerful chats.

Clouds wear shades, now that's a sight,
Tickling the sun, what pure delight!
Laughter spills from petal-lipped blooms,
As rainbows pop in silly rooms.

The Silent Orchard

In a grove where giggles hide,
Apples giggle, full of pride.
Cherries wearing bowties bright,
Wink at stars in the soft twilight.

Whispers float on the breeze,
Jokes are traded like sweet peas.
Crickets join in with a song,
In this orchard, laughter's strong.

Nectar of New Beginnings

The flowers tease the flitting bees,
Sipping nectar with such ease.
One froggy hops, bumps a bee,
"Hey, you missed a spot, look at me!"

The sun winks at all the fun,
As daisies dance with everyone.
Funny hats made of sunshine,
Make every day feel just divine.

Sprouting Dreams

Seeds take naps beneath the soil,
Dreaming up a grand recoil.
"It's sprouting time, let's all explode!"
Said the shy little bean, as it strode.

With a giggle and a twist,
Each little sprout cannot resist.
They tickle the toes of passing ants,
"Join our party, wear your pants!"

Flourishing Fantasies

A thought ran wild, oh what a chase,
Chasing rainbows in a jar of space.
Socks on my ears, a hat made of cheese,
Dancing with ducks in the warm spring breeze.

Bubble gum skies and jellybean trees,
Monkeys in suits sipping herbal teas.
I thought I'd catch wisdom, but caught a cold,
Now I wear a crown made of marigold.

A Spectrum of Spirits

A jellybean jumped from a cupboard high,
With a wink and a giggle, it soared through the sky.
Orange with polka dots, oh what a sight,
It danced with the clouds, a pure delight.

Tickling the sun with balloons in tow,
A parade of airships began to flow.
With laughter that echoed beyond the blue,
They painted the world in a riot of hue.

Unraveled Tapestries

Threads of imagination spill and unwind,
Tangled in laughter, a curious bind.
A shoelace snaked from my shoe in dismay,
While a peanut whispered, 'Let's dance today!'

Socks tossing popcorn under the table,
A cat in a tux, feeling quite stable.
We stitched dreams into quilts of bright thread,
And laughed till the moonlight glowed overhead.

Uplifted Realities

A carrot proclaimed, 'I'm a mighty knight!'
While a lettuce leaf chuckled in pure delight.
Together they galloped on spaghetti steeds,
Chasing jellyfish with whimsical needs.

Underneath rainbows, they played a sweet tune,
With whispers of cupcakes and lattes at noon.
Each giggle a sprinkle, each smile a burst,
In a land where reality's rules are reversed.

Canvas of Consciousness

In my head, a bright paint fight,
Colors clash, oh what a sight!
Thoughts like splatters on a wall,
A masterpiece or just a brawl?

Brushes dance on the mental stage,
Creating chaos, not a cage.
Silly dreams in vibrant hues,
Where logic's lost with all the blues.

Each idea, a wacky brush,
In this art, I find my rush.
Laughing at the mess I've made,
In this lovely thought parade!

So let the colors run amok,
In the moment, time is stuck.
Life's a canvas, so let's play,
With the thoughts that bloom today!

Flourishing Layers of Self

In layers thick, I wear my jests,
Like onions, oh, I must confess!
Peel one back, a giggle shows,
Another layer? Who knows, who knows!

Beneath the silly hats I wear,
Lies a joke, a silly dare.
With every layer, I unearth,
A side of me, oh, so much mirth!

Sometimes I'm deep, sometimes I'm light,
In this comedy, I take flight.
Cocooned in laughs, I stretch my wings,
Finding joy in all these things.

So here's to layers, thick and thin,
Where silly thoughts will always win.
In this joyful, goofy spree,
I'll bloom in layers, just let me be!

Afrocentrism in Bloom

Look at me, I spin and swirl,
With colors bright, watch them unfurl!
A hairdo tall, full of flair,
Each twist tells a story rare.

Dancing rhythms fill the air,
With every move, I shake my hair.
From roots so deep, I proudly rise,
A garden in my mind, no lies!

Pop and sizzle, here I stand,
With laughter blossoming, oh so grand.
Heritage blooms like flowers bright,
In this garden of pure delight.

So let us bloom, let spirits soar,
With unity, we'll dance and roar.
In every joke that we compose,
A radiant world of joy unfolds!

Fragrant Musings

In the garden of thoughts, a bee hums,
With silly ideas, like whipped cream plums.
A daisy just danced, forgot its own name,
While tulips giggle in a leafy game.

Sunshine tickles, clouds wear a grin,
A flower's best joke? 'You should see my twin!'
The roses gossip, petals all aflutter,
While daisies chime in, 'Did you hear that utter?'

Thoughts bloom like wildflowers, carefree and bright,
In this brainy garden, all wrongs feel right.
I try to remember where I put my shoe,
But the blossoms are laughing; it's a wacky crew.

With petals of wisdom, each stem a wise crack,
In this mind of mine, there's no need to hold back.
Every tumbleweed thought rolls off with a spin,
In this fragrant chaos, I revel within.

Blossoms of Insight

A tulip declared, 'I just found my muse!'
While daffodils ponder, 'Did we pay our dues?'
Funny how thoughts sprout, like weeds in the sun,
A chortle of laughter has already begun.

The marigolds whisper of plans for a play,
Where pansies wear costumes in a colorful fray.
'Why did the petunia bring a spoon?' they all ask,
'To stir up some trouble – that's quite the task!'

A thinker once tripped on a stray little sprout,
Shouted, 'Who knew, ideas could grow all about?'
With laughter and giggles, the cosmos conspire,
In the garden of thoughts, we bloom and retire.

So here's to the blossoms that brighten our day,
Funky and funny, they light up our way.
With petals like puzzles, each one a surprise,
Life's mystery solved under fluttering skies.

Vibrant Reflections

Mirror, mirror, what blooms today?
A sunflower's giggle, a bumblebee's sway.
The thoughts flit and flutter like butterflies bold,
In this wildflower patch, the stories unfold.

Chlorophyll thinkers with shades of delight,
Strike poses like models under moon's soft light.
A wise little fern cracked a joke so quirky,
'What do you call flowers who get too perky?'

They bloom in confusion, each petal a clown,
With thoughts that just tumble and roll on the ground.
The daisies are daisying, spreading their cheer,
With sprigs of laughter that tickle the ear.

Pondering petals, let silliness reign,
In this vibrant mindspace, we dance in the rain.
Each bloom tells a tale in a hue of pure fun,
Embracing our quirks, we bask in the sun.

Awakening the Inner Garden

Wake up, sleepy thoughts, let's start the day!
The lilies are snoring, but that's just their way.
A cactus in shades just cracked a small smile,
'You won't plant a prick, if you stay for a while!'

The veggie brigade is planning a feast,
Throwing a party, to say the least.
'What's our theme?' asked the sprout with a glee,
'Let's celebrate freshness, come join our spree!'

Thoughts sprout like radishes, all chubby and nice,
With quirky ideas, we mingle with spice.
As laughter erupts from the soil of our minds,
Every root and tendril uniquely entwined.

So dance through the rows where ideas take flight,
With a bounce and a wiggle, everything feels right.
In this inner garden where humor can grow,
We'll pluck at our worries, and let laughter flow.

Awakening Blossoms

In the garden of thoughts, flowers sprout,
Ideas dance around, there's laughter throughout.
A dandelion sneezes, pollen takes flight,
Sunflowers giggle, basking in light.

Tulips tell jokes that tickle the breeze,
While cacti play tag, dodging busy bees.
A rose tries to laugh but starts to blush,
School of fish gossip, all in a rush.

Petunias are pranking the daisies next door,
Winking and waggling, they always want more.
Cherry blossoms chuckle at squirrels so bold,
Their silly antics in stories retold.

Every petal holds humor, a secret surprise,
Where laughter and flowers harmoniously rise.
Nature's own jesters, vibrant and free,
In this blooming chaos, there's joy to see.

Nature of Reflection

In a pond of thought, frogs leap and croak,
They ponder life's mysteries and share a joke.
A fish swims by with a grin on its face,
Suggesting that stillness is just a rat race.

Butterflies stop for a tea party break,
Chatting with shadows, for goodness' sake!
The evening sun giggles, dips low for a peek,
While clouds float by, playing hide-and-seek.

A squirrel with glasses reads books by the shore,
Reciting old wisdom, wanting much more.
Trees nod in rhythm, their laughter aflame,
As wind teases branches, calling their name.

Reflections abound in nature's own cheer,
With whispers and giggles drifting near.
Among all the ripples, fun is the thread,
In this amusing world where thoughts are fed.

Unfurling Perspectives

A thinking cap worn by a curious bee,
Buzzing out questions, 'What's it like to be me?'
While daisies retort, with petals so wide,
'We've seen the world through a dewdrop's slide.'

Worms beneath giggle, unpacking their dreams,
Contemplating life while sipping on streams.
Grasshoppers debate the best way to hop,
With laughter echoing, they just can't stop.

Even the rocks share their solid views,
While crickets chat joyfully, sipping on dew.
A wise old turtle grumbles with flair,
'Perspective's a treasure; just take the time to care.'

In this garden of thought, humor's the key,
Opening doors to new ways we can see.
As petals unwrap and the giggles unfold,
Unfurling ideas, both silly and bold.

Radiant Epiphanies

A sunbeam tickles the back of a cat,
Which leaps and plays, just imagine that!
Where light bulbs pop in a flower's head,
Each bloom bursts with laughter, painting the spread.

'What if,' says one petal, 'we danced in the rain?'
While daisies debate if they'll grow tall or wane.
A blushing bud says, 'Let's just break free,
Who knew that thinking could be this silly?'

Caterpillars giggle with dreams of the sky,
As they flutter about on a leafy high fry.
Amidst all the bloom and humorous whirls,
Life is a circus with such silly twirls.

In each radiant moment, an epiphany flies,
From daisies to roses, beneath fluffy skies.
With laughter and joy, they sing all night,
In this jolly old garden, life's pure delight.

Verdant Landscapes of the Mind

In fields of green where hedgehogs dance,
A squirrel in tights takes a bold chance.
Thoughts like daisies sprout and sway,
In this garden, who needs a bouquet?

Whimsical breezes tease the scene,
Dancing with butterflies, so serene.
My brain's a jungle, wild and free,
Chasing down giggles like honeybee.

A flamingo wearing shades struts tall,
He knows when to trip, he knows when to call.
Ideas bloom like popcorn in the air,
Dip your toes in, but beware the bear!

With laughter and light, the weeds are fun,
In this grassy maze, let's run and run.
What's that, a raccoon with a mustache?
In this mind's eye, nothing is trash.

Sunlit Thoughts

Under the rays where silly shines,
Thoughts bubble up like fizzy lines.
Sunflower smiles, spreading their cheer,
Chasing the shadows, come dance here!

Clouds made of cotton candy fluff,
Tickling our brains, oh, isn't it tough?
Each giggle a spark, each thought a light,
In sunlit laughter, we take flight.

A rabbit in glasses reads a book,
While pondering why the chicken crooks.
In wonderland, the humor's grand,
Twists and turns, just like a band.

In warmth of the sun, ideas drip sweet,
Like syrupy moonlight on popcorn treat.
We paint the sky with colors of fun,
In our quirky playground, all are welcome to run!

Ephemeral Blossoms

Petals burst forth with a giggle and pop,
They twirl in the breeze, then quickly drop.
Thoughts like fireworks, brief but bright,
In twilight gardens, they take flight.

A cactus tips its hat, quite bemused,
At the chaos of thoughts that we've confused.
With butterflies whispering secrets near,
We laugh at the punchlines - so sincere!

Oh, the quicksilver dreams that dart around,
Leapfrogging logic, never quite found.
Ephemeral blooms, a riotous show,
Who knew the mind could put on such a glow?

Tulips shout jokes while daisies laugh loud,
Their petals are jokes made to please the crowd.
In the flower bed where whimsy grows,
Each thought's a cheer, wherever it goes.

Cultivated Whispers

In rows of whispers, ideas take root,
A witty melon dons a bowtie suit.
With each gentle chuckle, the seeds take flight,
They sprout into stories, pure delight.

Gardens of giggles in fanciful beds,
Grown by the jester, with floppy hats and threads.
Each vine entangles a satirical tune,
Making peace with a dancing raccoon.

Underneath moonlight, the carrots recite,
Their thoughts on why potatoes just don't ignite.
Laughter flows freely like wine in the sun,
In this world of whimsy, we're all just one.

With plump tomatoes winking with glee,
And pumpkins that roll just to say "Whee!"
In cultivated whispers, the mind's a fair game,
Where jokes blossom endlessly, ripe with fame.

Cerebral Canopy

Underneath the brainy trees,
Thoughts dangle like ripe bananas.
I swing in circles, feeling free,
Chasing dreams like jungle iguanas.

Ideas flutter, swoop, and dive,
Like squirrels on a caffeine spree.
Every notion comes alive,
In this wild, wacky canopy.

Bouncing brainwaves, silly sight,
Logic wears a clownish hat.
Give my neurons a little bite,
For comic gold, they're where it's at!

Giggles echo through the leaves,
As wisdom does a funny dance.
Life's a joke, or so it weaves,
In this cerebral expanse!

Echoes of Growth

Whispers bounce from thought to thought,
Like rubber balls in a gym.
Each quirky idea's dearly bought,
And some just might be quite dim!

In the garden of my brain,
The veggies all are wearing socks.
Brains prance like they're on a train,
Dancing 'round the paradox.

Every giggle sparks delight,
As flowers wear their tinfoil hats.
Serious minds can take a flight,
While others chase some dancing cats!

Echoes of growth paint the sky,
With colors bright and joy to share.
A thought just noted, oh my my,
Who knew brains could be this rare?

Flourish in Silence

In quiet corners, thoughts will bloom,
Like mushrooms in a secret room.
The mind does jive in muted glee,
Unplugged from chaos, feeling free.

With jokes that sprout like daisies fair,
In silence, cackles fill the air.
Smart cracks bloom like flowers do,
The quieter, the funnier too!

Imagine brains in a retreat,
With each odd thought a tasty treat.
Laughter grows in double time,
While intellect performs its rhyme.

So let's embrace this laugh-filled grace,
As neurons dance in a funny space.
In quietude, we break the mold,
With jokes that never get too old!

Bloom of Intellect

A brain with blooms is quite a sight,
Thoughts sprouting flowers, bold and bright.
A cactus wearing spectacles,
Lines of wisdom in silly pixels.

Bees buzzing round each wacky thought,
Honeyed ideas, can't be bought.
In this garden of sheer delight,
Every pun takes wing in flight!

Intellect flourishes with flair,
Twirling thoughts in gusts of air.
Laughter echoes, roots entwined,
In the garden of the mind!

So join the show where intellect's grand,
With blooms shaped like a rubber band.
Through every twist and zany plot,
Our minds will laugh, oh what a lot!

Whispers of a Growth Heart

In my head, ideas play,
Like squirrels on a sunny day.
They bounce around, then take a leap,
I giggle as they play hide and seek.

Thoughts sprout up, a wild vine,
Some stick around, some are just fine.
But oh, the ones that make me grin,
Are those absurd, where do I begin?

With each bizarre and silly scheme,
I chase them down like a racing dream.
They twist and turn, they laugh and tease,
Creating chaos, oh, what a breeze!

So here's to thoughts that dance and twirl,
To every twist, each silly swirl.
Laughter blooms in my crowded mind,
In this garden, joys are intertwined.

Ideas in Full Blossom

Petals made of giggles grow,
In the garden of my thoughts, you know.
Ideas bloom like daisies bright,
Causing chuckles in morning light.

Here's a notion dressed in flair,
A funny hat, a grouchy bear.
They pop up like popcorn in a pan,
Bouncing around, oh yes they can!

Each wild thought, a sprightly race,
Like a clam in a comical chase.
They blossom into jokes and puns,
Turning plain days into funny runs.

So let's celebrate this mental spree,
With laughter as sweet as can be.
In the vineyard of my whirly mind,
Every giggle is uniquely designed.

Cultivating Creativity

In my mind's patch, seeds are sown,
Whimsical thoughts have brightly grown.
They dance like flowers on a breeze,
Stirring up joy with the greatest ease.

Chasing rainbows in my head,
Some thoughts are zany, some are dread.
A monster holding a pizza slice,
Who knew veggies could be so nice?

I plant my dreams, they sprout and shout,
Creativity blooms, there's no doubt.
With laughter spreading through each vein,
I reap the harvest of goofy grain.

So here's to all the ideas spry,
With each one, I let out a sigh.
In this garden of quips and quirks,
My heart finds joy in playful works.

A Garden of Dreams

In the soil of imagination's delight,
Funny thoughts take their flight.
Each one grows, bizarre and bright,
Painting my world in pure light.

A cow in patterned socks will dance,
While trees wear hats, given the chance.
They sway and giggle in sunny cheer,
Creating a spectacle, oh so clear!

My garden boasts of puns galore,
Like ducks in tuxedos, there's so much more.
Each blooming joke, a vibrant hue,
Flourishing in laughter, oh how they grew!

So wander down this comical lane,
With whimsical dreams that entertain.
In the fields of joy, my spirit beams,
Amidst the riches of funny themes.

Budding Horizons

In the garden of thoughts, ideas sprout,
Like daisies in spring, they wiggle about.
A thought takes a tumble, oh what a sight,
It trips on a pun and giggles with delight.

Mind's a wild party, with snacks on the floor,
Jokes played by neurons, who could ask for more?
A tumbleweed rolls in, wearing a grin,
Shouting, 'Hey folks, let the fun begin!'

Silly concepts bloom with a splash of cheer,
Dancing like flowers, in bright atmosphere.
Thoughts prance and jive, a whimsical crew,
Each one more outrageous than the last few.

So plant those silly seeds and let them grow,
In fields of laughter, watch the humor flow.
With every new quirk, a story to tell,
In this garden of giggles, we flourish so well.

Nurtured Notions

Nurtured notions bob like corks on the sea,
They giggle like children, wild and carefree.
One floats on by, wearing mismatched shoes,
Chasing rare thoughts like an enthusiastic muse.

In the pot of my mind, they're brewing up fun,
Like coffee with sprinkles, or chocolate with sun.
A notion starts dancing, all jiggly and bright,
Saying, 'I'm the winner of the wittiest fight!'

Whimsical wonders with giggles galore,
Knocking on doors, saying, 'Just one more!'
So let's water these dreams with laughter today,
As we nurture the funny in all we convey.

A garden of joy, sprouting silly sights,
Where every wild notion really takes flight.
With humor our sunshine, and whimsy our rain,
The more we delight, the more we'll gain!

Petal Pathways

Petals of laughter flutter all around,
On paths of whimsical thoughts, where joy is found.
Each step's an adventure, a giggle or two,
Where puns toss and turn like a dance at the zoo.

Winding through flowers, all dressed up in jokes,
Where silliness blossoms, amidst friendly folks.
A daffodil chuckles, while blooms do the twist,
Saying, 'You must admit, I'm too cute to resist!'

Paths strewn with puns, like confetti in spring,
Where rainbows of mirth make the heart want to sing.
As concepts unfold like a page in a book,
Each turn brings a smile, a joyous new look.

So scamper through petals, make memories bright,
In gardens of giggles, where day hugs the night.
With laughter as fuel, we'll stroll ever free,
On pathways of whimsy, just you wait and see!

Vibrations of Enlightenment

In the orchestra of thoughts, a symphony plays,
With each note of wisdom, hilarity sways.
Tickling the senses with bubbles of cheer,
Where enlightenment's dance brings the funny near.

Vibrations of laughter, like waves in the breeze,
Whistling sweet melodies from tall ancient trees.
A squirrel strums chords on a violin string,
While the wisdom imparted makes the heart sing.

Jokes bounce like raindrops on rooftops above,
Creating a tapestry woven with love.
As insights take flight, and silliness reigns,
In the land of the bright, joy freely gains.

So ride on the waves, let the humor explode,
In this concert of quirks, where happiness flowed.
With each point of light, a smile takes flight,
Embracing the magic that dances at night.

Inflorescence of Dreams

In a world of jumbled schemes,
Where laughter flows like streams,
Thoughts like balloons take flight,
Chasing giggles through the night.

Silly critters play hide and seek,
Whispering secrets, cheek to cheek,
With each burst of brilliant fun,
Dreams unfurl, all said and done.

Arboretum of Thoughts

In this forest of whacky views,
Trees wear hats, and squirrels snooze,
Branches jiggle with delight,
While wisdom walks a tightrope, light.

Leaves exchange a gleeful wink,
Just as flowers start to think,
What if thoughts could dance and spin?
And wear polka dots and grin?

Whimsical Wildflowers

Here in fields of vibrant glee,
Wildflowers dream of being free,
They twirl and sway with silly grace,
Tickling bees in friendly race.

Each petal holds a joke or two,
A punny riddle, just for you,
Blooming joy in colors bright,
A comic strip of pure delight.

Garden of Enlightenment

In this patch, ideas grow,
Sunshine laughs at thoughts in tow,
Gnomes recite their ancient prose,
While daisies plot their comedy shows.

Rabbits knitting socks with flair,
Bumblebees become the mayor,
Every corner a new surprise,
Where wisdom wears a clown disguise.

Seeds of Inspiration

In a garden where ideas sprout,
My thoughts play tag, they jump about.
With daisies of dreams and roses of fun,
I laugh as I chase the thoughts that run.

A sprinkle of giggles, a dash of cheer,
Whimsical wonders dance near.
Like weeds that refuse to be contained,
My mind's a circus, fully unchained.

Sowing jokes in fertile ground,
The funniest seedlings all around.
I tickle the petals, watch them grin,
As laughter blooms, let the games begin.

With each thought's color, my canvas expands,
Crafting a bouquet with my clumsy hands.
Oh, the hilarity that grows and grows,
In this wild garden, anything goes!

Vivid Visions Ascend

My mind's a balloon, it floats so high,
Chasing butterflies, oh my, oh my!
A parade of colors, bold and bright,
A dancing rainbow in sheer delight.

Thoughts are like popcorn, popping all around,
Each kernel, a giggle, a funny sound.
I'm wearing spectacles covered in goo,
So who knows what visions might come into view?

With googly eyes and oversized shoes,
I leap through the clouds, with nothing to lose.
Each twist and turn, a rollercoaster ride,
In this amusement park, I take pride.

Spinning in circles, laughter's my guide,
I twirl with ideas, let whimsy decide.
Up, up and away, my thoughts take flight,
In this vivid world, everything's light!

Echoes of Enlightenment

In the chamber of chuckles, wisdom rings,
As I ponder the meaning of silly things.
Enlightenment tickles, with whimsy it thrives,
Through echoes of laughter, I come alive.

With puns like butterflies that flutter and roam,
My thoughts start to dance, making themselves at home.
Each giggle a sparkle, a witty reply,
As the echoes of fun make the serious fly.

A light bulb goes off, but it's fuzzy, you see,
Creating more shadows than clarity!
Yet wisdom's peculiar, it rides on a joke,
In the hall of hilarity, we're all just folks.

Finding the humor, I stumble and trip,
On the path of enlightenment, I take a wild leap.
As laughter reverberates, a comical tune,
Echoes of joy under the light of the moon.

Unfurling Potential

Like a burrito bursting with tasty delight,
My mind unrolls thoughts, what a silly sight!
Each layer of laughter, wrapped tight with a twist,
I savor the flavors, I can't resist.

As ideas unfold like origami swans,
I giggle and hiccup at all of their yawns.
From the folds I create, a parade begins,
Marching forth boldly, with cackles and grins.

Each twist of my brain, like a pretzel so grand,
Creating more knots, but I find it unplanned.
With every unchecked whim, I break from the mold,
Unfurling my laughter, wild and bold.

In this circus of thoughts, a real riot,
My potential erupts; come join the diet!
Where chuckles nourish and ideas take flight,
Unfurling my joy, from day into night.

A Field of Enlightenment

In a garden where thoughts dance and play,
Ideas sprout like weeds on a sunny day.
A flower in my head, oh what a sight,
It giggles and wiggles, such pure delight.

Petals of nonsense, blooming with cheer,
A sunflower whispers, "Come gather near!"
With bees of confusion, they sip the fun,
Pollinating laughter, oh how we've spun!

A tulip has a joke, oh how it teases,
While violets plan a party that never ceases.
In this patch of curiosity, we all collide,
Every quirky thought is a wild joyride.

So pluck a notion, give it a whirl,
In this field of folly, let creativity twirl.
Nature's canvas painted, pure and bright,
In the midst of the madness, oh what a sight!

Whispers of Vitality

A dandelion tickles my nose with a grin,
As it shares wild secrets, where do I begin?
The grass starts to giggle, a ticklish debate,
While daisies declare it's never too late.

Chirpy little thoughts flutter like a fly,
They bounce and they bounce, oh my, oh my!
With butterflies giggling, they chase with glee,
"Catch me if you can!" they call to the bee.

Hopping around like a curious weed,
Each notion's a laugh, that's all that we need.
In this circus of blooms, oh the joy we find,
A blooming parade in our whimsical mind.

So gather your laughter, let the flowers talk,
As we frolic together on this vibrant block.
In the whispers of life, let's spark a delight,
For in every small chuckle, the world's shining bright!

Kaleidoscope of Ideas

Through a prism of petals, ideas refract,
Colors of nonsense, and that's a known fact.
Each hue a thought, bright and absurd,
Swirling in giggles, barely a word.

There's lavender logic and rose-colored dreams,
With orchids of whimsy bursting at the seams.
A rainbow of humor, in chaos they bloom,
Lighting up paths with a sprinkle of zoom.

Tulips in tutus, prancing around,
Tickling each idea till they're lost, then found.
In nature's own circus, where wits intertwine,
Every silly thought is a sparkling sign.

So step into this garden of colorful cheer,
Where every mischief makes laughter appear.
In this kaleidoscope world, join the jam,
For what's better than laughter? Why, nothing, ma'am!

Botanical Reverie

In a whimsical jungle where giggles abound,
Ideas swing wildly from branch to the ground.
A humor vine wraps, tickling my toes,
As the roots of laughter take hold and they grow.

Ferns whisper puns to the daisies so bold,
While sunflowers chuckle, or so I'm told.
A botanist grins as ideas take flight,
With every new bloom comes a fresh comic light.

A cactus joins in with prickles of fun,
While primroses giggle, "Let's all run!"
In this garden of jest, we stumble and trip,
Each fallen thought is a joyful quip.

So wander these meadows where laughter gives chase,
In this leafy dreamland, find your own space.
For every new idea is a laugh worth pursuing,
In our botanical dreams, the joy keeps renewing!

Blooming Reflections

In a garden of thoughts, laughter grows,
Each idea a giggle, as the breezy wind blows.
I ponder like a flower, a bit askew,
Petals of nonsense, in a whimsical hue.

Mirror, mirror, why so bright?
I can't decide, am I wrong or right?
A dandelion's wisdom, in a ticklish gust,
Twirling and spinning, oh what a must!

Thoughts sprout wildly, like weeds in spring,
Some serious, some silly, oh what joy they bring.
I debate with my shadows, they always agree,
Together we chuckle, just like the bee.

So here in my mind, where the humor flows,
Laughter's a flower, and my heart it grows.
With a petal of fun, I stand in full view,
In a garden of giggles, I relish the brew.

Glistening Seeds

Sprouting like peas in a funny little pod,
Ideas bounce around, isn't life odd?
With a sprinkle of wit and a splash of cheer,
These glistening seeds, oh, they tickle the ear.

Each thought is a raindrop, plopping with glee,
Splashing in puddles, come dance with me!
They jump in a swirl, these merry old seeds,
Giggling together, fulfilling their needs.

Planting a vision, oh what a sight,
Giggling grasshoppers join in the delight.
Each seed finds a rhythm, a hilarious beat,
In the garden of folly, it's never offbeat.

So water the laughs, let the sunshine rise,
With roots of good humor, surprise, and skies.
The laughter will bloom, it's a joyful decree,
In the glistening garden, come join the spree!

Vines of Wisdom

Twisting and turning, like thoughts in my head,
Vines of funny wisdom, where silliness led.
Climbing to heights where the quirks intertwine,
Every clever quip is like sipping fine wine.

Bouncing and bobbing, my ideas take flight,
A monkey on a vine, oh what a sight!
Swinging through humor, I mimic the sun,
The brighter the laughter, the more I have fun.

With tendrils of jest, I explore spider webs,
Wisdom wrapped tight, like a grape on its ebb.
Each twist tells a story, each curl a good joke,
Oh, the vines of life—how they giggle and poke!

So let's climb together, share a hearty cheer,
With roots deeply planted, we'll conquer our fear.
In this jungle of thoughts, we'll dance and we'll play,
The vines of wisdom weave humor each day.

A Canvas of Growth

On a canvas of laughter, I paint with delight,
Colors of nonsense splash day and night.
Brushstrokes of giggles, in hues all around,
Creating a masterpiece, where smiles abound.

A sunbeam of humor lights up the scene,
Each stroke tells a joke, quite sly and serene.
With splashes of joy, I blend all the hues,
Mirthful creations, with tales to amuse.

Mixing my colors, I dance with the light,
A palette of chuckles, everything feels right.
Each shade a silly memory, bold and bright,
This canvas of growth is a whimsical sight.

So come take a peek at this fabulous art,
Where laughter is crafted straight from the heart.
In a world full of giggles, we'll all find our place,
On this canvas of humor, we'll share a huge space.

Fractals of Thought

Ideas dance like fractals bright,
Twisting and turning in pure delight.
Thoughts multiply like rabbits in spring,
Can't catch a one, but what joy they bring!

In my head, they spin and collide,
A circus of neurons, they won't hide.
Grab a thought, it's a slippery fish,
Serve it with laughter, that's my wish!

Like a kaleidoscope of giggles galore,
Each whimsy a key, unlocking the door.
What will I conjure? It's anyone's game,
Just don't ask logic—I've lost her name!

In this garden of jumbled jest,
Silly little ideas never rest.
Fractals of thought, a chaotic spree,
Who knew my brain could throw such a tea?

Echoing Aspirations

I whisper dreams to the garden breeze,
Watch them flutter like leaves on trees.
They bounce around, a funny old crew,
Taking detours, they don't have a clue.

Oh, aspirations, mildly absurd,
Like ducks in tuxedos, so very disturbed.
They quack and they waddle, with grand parade,
Even the moon thinks they've gone half-blade!

Each echo a chuckle, a resonant rhyme,
Frolicking freely, defying all time.
What's next on the list? Can't quite recall,
But I bet it involves juggling a wall!

Through fields of nonsense, my hopes take flight,
A cartoonish ride, oh what a sight!
Echoing aspirations, let laughter ring,
In the circus of dreams, I am the king!

Nurtured Notions

In the land of ideas, I plant some seeds,
Watering whims with giggles and needs.
Up pops a nonsense, a quirky old sprout,
Who knew that a tickle could help it out?

Nurtured notions like puppies in play,
Bounding around in a wild ballet.
What's that one doing? Oh dear, oh my!
It's trying to high-five a butterfly!

They bloom into plots rich and absurd,
My pet thoughts are saying the silliest words.
Laughs and snickers, a cacophony bright,
In my imagination, everything's right.

So let's water the laughter, and wind the fun,
These nurtured notions have only begun.
With a sprinkle of joy and a splash of cheer,
They'll bloom like a rainbow, oh my dear!

Dreamweaver's Grove

Welcome to the grove where daydreams dance,
They trip on the roots, but don't mind the chance.
With laughter as syrup on wobbling trees,
They giggle and sway in the gentle breeze.

In this twisted forest of whimsical zest,
Each thought is a fruit; they're best for the jest.
Pluck one and munch, oh what a surprise!
Tastes like a jig that jumps in your eyes!

Dreamweavers spinning in wacky delight,
Crafting absurdities deep into night.
With brushstrokes of fun, they'll color the sky,
Painting old stars that just want to fly.

So wander with glee in this curious glade,
Where laughter and joy are merrily made.
Dreamweaver's grove, let your spirit soar,
In this fantastic land, you'll ask for more!

Tapestry of Aspirations

A dream with polka dots, how fine,
I painted it with lemon-lime.
It danced like jelly on a spoon,
In a world where cows can croon.

With wishes stitched on neon threads,
It flutters like a chorus of beds.
Oh, aspirations, quirky and bright,
You tickle my brain, what a sight!

Fertile Horizons

Oh, the fields that stretch and sway,
Where thoughts sprout like weeds in May.
My brain's a farm with no fence tight,
Harvesting giggles, oh, what a sight!

With thoughts as ripe as watermelon,
I juggle dreams like a circus felon.
The sunbeam's giggle warms my soul,
On fertile ground, I find my goal.

Flourishing Thoughts

Thoughts bloom like flowers in a hat,
Each petal giggles, 'imagine that!'
Dancing on air with a sparkly grin,
They whisper nonsense, let the fun begin.

My mind's a garden, wild and free,
Where cereal sings with glee.
Thoughts sprout legs and start to prance,
Inviting laughter to join the dance!

Petals of Imagination

In the jar of my mind, ideas twist,
Like spaghetti that can't resist.
Each noodle curls, a silly sight,
Petals of thoughts, in neon light.

They flutter and flutter like butterflies,
With googly eyes and rainbow ties.
Oh, the whimsy in each little pluck,
In the garden of giggles, I'm out of luck!

Flourish in the Quiet

In a garden of thoughts, I found my muse,
Whispering secrets, refusing to snooze.
Giggling flowers sway to a silly song,
Tickling my brain, it feels so wrong!

A cactus with jokes, sharp wit at play,
Telling punchlines that ruin my day.
Bumblebees buzzing with comedic flair,
Each bloom a laugh, as I sit in my chair.

Petals with puns dropping down like rain,
I'm rolling in giggles, can't help but complain.
Butterflies fluttering, dancing around,
My thoughts, in this humor, are blissfully found.

The sun winks at shadows stretching so wide,
As I chuckle at critters with nowhere to hide.
In this vibrant chaos, my mind does play neat,
Each bloom brings a smile, it's quite the treat!

Harvesting the Soul's Palette

In a field of giggles, I pluck out the wise,
Tangled vines twist, hide behind laughter's guise.
Colors so vivid, they dance on my tongue,
Jokes ripe for the picking, to everyone sung.

Each berry I munch spills forth ticklish grins,
Making puns bloom like the wildest of sins.
Veggies with voices, oh what a delight,
They argue on veggies, but all in good light.

With carrots in bow ties and peas on parade,
A salad of humor, I'm perfectly made.
While radishes chuckle, the corn joins the fun,
This harvest of laughter has only begun.

Sunset arrives, the jokes hit their peak,
As the moonlight giggles, it's laughter I seek.
In this quirky garden where thoughts intertwine,
Every chuckle and snicker is simply divine!

Dappled Thoughts Dancing

Under leafy canopies, thoughts twist and twirl,
Where laughter's a stream, and chaos does swirl.
Silly shadows skip, with hats made of sun,
Cheerful confetti, oh boy, this is fun!

Dances of dappled light, clowning around,
Hiding behind twigs where humor is found.
Squirrels in spectacles plan their next trick,
Juggling acorns while I watch, oh so quick.

Laughter erupts, like bubbles in air,
Chasing my worries, without a care.
Twirling in circles with daisies on hand,
A dance of the mind, I won't misunderstand.

In vivid imaginations, we prance and we play,
Mischievous dreams spill like paint on the gray.
Joycolored thoughts bounce, like pops in a feast,
In this madcap ballet, I'm laughing the least!

Budding Brilliance

Tiny buds whisper, ideas take flight,
Sprouting their laughter in morning's soft light.
Jokes seed in silence, then burst forth with glee,
As petals of wisdom play peekaboo with me.

Each bud a surprise, tickles to explore,
Spoiling for giggles, they shout, "Give us more!"
A daisy with mischief, a rose full of wit,
Even the shy violets refuse to sit.

Sunshine and chuckles play games in the breeze,
While silly little sprouts bend down on their knees.
Stretching for joy, like a beam from the sun,
It's a riot of brilliance, let the fun run.

In this garden of laughter, where thoughts roam so free,
Every bloom is a riddle, come chuckle with me.
With each little sprout, new giggles unwind,
In the joy of all colors, there's wisdom to find!

Mindscapes in Color

In a garden of thoughts, I wear my tints,
Chasing rainbows while my logic hints.
Colors burst forth, like laughter in spring,
Spilling out jokes that my neurons fling.

Daffodils giggle, tulips tease,
As daisies dance on a gentle breeze.
Petals of puns float through my brain,
Tickling my senses, a joyous refrain.

Brainwaves bouncing, bright and bold,
Sketching dreams in colors untold.
I scribble in shades of cherry and lime,
Painting my verses, oh what a rhyme!

With every thought that blooms and twirls,
A vibrant parade of imagination swirls.
Crowning my mind with a riot of hues,
A tapestry doused in whimsy and views.

Cerebral Petal Pusher

In the garden of notions, I plant a joke,
Watering laughter with each quirky poke.
Sowing the seeds of wit in my mind,
Watch as the blossoms of humor unwind.

The daisies chatter, the roses roar,
A chorus of giggles, forever more.
Each petal whispers a story or two,
With brains like bees buzzing, it's all true!

Sprouting ideas in funky shapes,
Turning my thoughts into playful drapes.
I'm a petal peddler, come take a stroll,
As the flowers unfold their hilarious role.

With cerebellum in bloom, I design,
A carnival of quirkiness that's genuinely mine.
Each thought a bloom that twists and spins,
In this bouncy patch where the laughter begins.

Unleashing Inner Flora

In the depths of my mind, a garden awaits,
Where giggles grow tall and silliness mates.
Sprouts of ideas burst forth with a grin,
Each chuckle-a-plant, my inner mind's kin.

A sunflower nods with a wink and a spin,
While lollipops bloom on a satin-soft skin.
Buds of giggles shoot up from the ground,
As humor and cleverness frolic around.

With petals that tickle, and stems that sway,
I wander through thoughts like a playful bouquet.
A joke on the vine, I pick it with glee,
Hoping one tickles the funny in me.

In this playful patch, I dance with delight,
My mind blooming brightly, oh what a sight!
With laughter as rain and joy as the sun,
I unleash my inner flora; let's have some fun!

Tapestry of Thoughts

A quilt of ideas, stitched with a smile,
Threads of absurdity, layered in style.
Each stitch a giggle, each patch a jest,
Woven together, this is my best.

Fabrics of whimsy in colors so bright,
A tapestry gifted with pure delight.
I'll tie every thought with a pun's gentle swoop,
Creating a canvas where the chuckles loop.

With buttons of laughter, I adorn my mind,
Sewing up giggles that are one of a kind.
Every thread tells a tale that's silly and sweet,
A cover of joy in my mental retreat.

So come, take a peek at this playful art,
Where humor and whimsy play every part.
In this cozy patchwork, I find my way,
Embracing the laughter of each funny day.

Mossy Footsteps of Thought

In the garden of brain, where ideas roam free,
Thoughts jump like frogs, oh so silly to see.
They hop on to lilies, take a curious dive,
Wearing little hats, just to feel alive.

Daisies chat gossip behind a tall tree,
"Did you hear the one about the bumblebee?"
He claimed he could sing, but he squeaked like a mouse,
And danced with a shoehorn found under the house.

Clouds laugh at shadows that stretch on the ground,
As giggling squirrels play hide-and-seek all around.
Each corner of sunshine brings whispers of cheer,
And tickles the mind in a way we hold dear.

So dance with your memories, swirl with delight,
Let the mossy footsteps guide through the night.
For in this mind jungle, adventure's in store,
With every thought blossoming like never before.

A Garden of Whimsy

In a patch of bright thoughts, where giggles do bloom,
The flowers wear spectacles, avoiding the gloom.
A gopher named Greg plays tag with a snail,
While dancing on daisies, without fear of fail.

Butterflies debate wearing polka dots bright,
While worms in tuxedos discuss grace with delight.
The grass tickles toes as they trip on a dream,
Where laughter is sprinkled like sugar on cream.

An octopus juggles some peaches on stage,
While the sun plays the lute, turning every page.
The daisies clink glasses with daisies a mile,
In the garden of whimsy, you can't help but smile.

So wander through thoughts that are playful and light,
Let whimsy lead you on this magical flight.
For each turn of the mind is a giggly surprise,
A garden of laughter where nonsense can rise.

Petal-Powered Dreams

In the corridors of sleep, where the flowers take flight,
Petal-powered dreams whirl in the soft moonlight.
A tulip dons sneakers, ready to race,
While daisies in tutus perform with such grace.

The garden's alive with scents that amuse,
As honeysuckles gossip and share the good news.
Bees buzz in tune as the daisies sway,
In a dance-off of petals to brighten the day.

Sunflowers gossip while sipping their tea,
"Did you hear about Charlie? He danced with a bee!"
Petals play tag with the breeze in a whirl,
In this realm of the mind, let your fantasies twirl.

So tiptoe through dreams that are silly and sweet,
With petal-powered thoughts that can't be beat.
Each bloom holds a secret, a giggle to share,
In a world made of laughter, beyond all compare.

Mosaic of Intellect

A patchwork of ideas, bright pieces of thought,
Crafted with humor, with laughter as sought.
Puzzles of nonsense sit snug on the shelf,
While the mind's jigsaw dances, just being itself.

A wise old owl with a monocle grins,
Watching squirrels in suits spinning tales of their wins.
"Why did the acorn take flight?" he quips with a laugh,
"To prove he could soar, not just be a half!"

The butterflies gather, a council for fun,
Negotiating giggles 'til the day is done.
Each morsel of insight a colorful thread,
In this quirky design where all laughter is spread.

So piece together laughter, a mosaic so bright,
With strokes of absurd that dance in the light.
For the mind is a canvas, forever in play,
Creating a masterpiece day after day.

The Flowering Soul

In a garden of thoughts, I do twirl,
Where daisies of dreams begin to unfurl.
I plant every question like seeds in the air,
And hope they sprout answers, funny and rare.

The roses of laughter bloom bright in my head,
With petals of puns dancing 'round like a thread.
Tulips poke fun as they sway in the breeze,
While daffodils giggle, promising cheese!

Bees buzzing jokes as they pollinate wise,
Creating honeyed laughter beneath sunny skies.
The garden's alive with whimsical cheer,
As wisdom grows sweeter, year after year.

So tend to your thoughts, let them sprout and roll,
In this patch of the psyche, there's joy in the soul.
Pull weeds of the worry and nurture the jest,
For the flowering heart is truly the best!

Cultivating Curiosity

With a trowel of wonder, I dig for a clue,
In the plot of my mind, where odd questions stew.
What if cats wore hats, and dogs danced in shoes?
The more I imagine, the more I amuse!

I water my thoughts with a sprinkle of glee,
And watch as the wild ideas blossom like me.
A garden of queries, oh look at them grow,
From tiny absurdities sprouting a show!

The carrots have comments, the pumpkins, big dreams,
Each vegetable whispering silly extremes.
As I harvest the laughter, I chuckle with pride,
For curiosity's garden is a fun-loving ride!

So plant all your wonders, let oddities bloom,
In the field of your brain, there's always more room.
With every new question, the laughter can sprout,
In the sunshine of folly, there's never a doubt!

Vibrant Visions

With colors of chaos splashed on my mind,
I sketch out horizons where humor's unlined.
A splash of a giggle, a dash of a grin,
In vibrant imaginings, fun chaos begins!

Swirling in colors, the jests take to flight,
Where oranges chat with the blues every night.
A carnival of thoughts, where the silly roam free,
In the land of the whimsical, I find the key!

Each brushstroke a chuckle, each line a small laugh,
As I paint my ideas upon this bright path.
With canary tales and a canvas of rhyme,
These visions of laughter are truly sublime!

So gather your colors and twist life's design,
Let the vibrant laughter in your heart align.
For in this playful art, joy is the theme,
As wild and as wacky as a daydream!

Efflorescence of Wisdom

In the orchard of thoughts, ripe wisdom does bloom,
With each funny quirk, it dispels all the gloom.
A punchline of learning, what a surprising blend,
Where the fruit of the mind is both funny and friend!

I pluck berries of insight, juicy and bright,
Sweet with a hint of a humorous bite.
With each laughter-filled morsel, I savor the fun,
Who knew thought could blossom under the sun?

The trees laugh with giggles, their branches all sway,
As jokes rain like blossoms, come what may.
Every leaf whispers wisdom, wrapped up in a jest,
In this garden of laughter, I'm truly the best!

So treasure those thoughts that make you delight,
For wisdom is sweet when it's wrapped up in light.
Let jokes burst like flowers, let lessons be bold,
In the efflorescence of laughter, wisdom unfolds!

Awakening Ideas

On a Monday morning, ideas awake,
Dancing around like a cake at a bake.
They bounce like bunnies, oh what a sight,
Wearing itsy-bitsy hats, feeling just right.

Thoughts sprout up like weeds in a row,
Each one quirkier, putting on a show.
With giggles and chuckles, they play tag,
While scribbling on napkins, they never lag.

Brain cells in jammies, having a spree,
Plotting world takeovers, oh what a spree!
Ideas like popcorn, they pop and they crack,
Watch out! Here comes one—a wild snack attack.

As sunshine peeks through, they take a leap,
Jumping in puddles, oh, what a heap!
With laughter and joy, they run out the door,
Awakening thoughts—who could ask for more!

Flourishing Dreams

Dreams take a stroll on a grassy hill,
With butterflies twirling, they get their thrill.
Tiptoeing past clouds, wearing pajamas,
Munching on marshmallows, oh, what a drama!

Chasing the rainbows,: oh, what a chase,
Silly little thoughts, come join the race!
With squeaks and giggles, they leap through the air,
Surfing on starlight without a care.

Each moment is fizzy, like soda pop,
Bubbles bursting forth as the laughter won't stop.
In a land made of whims, where dreams get a boost,
They dance on the paths where creativity's juiced.

With silly hats topped off with sprightly tunes,
They're itching to fly like bright, soaring moons.
In the gardens of laughter, dreams grow so tall,
Flourishing whimsies—we're having a ball!

Seeds of Imagination

Seeds of sweet ideas, all lined up in a row,
Planted with care by the sun's gentle glow.
Watered with laughter, and sprinkled with glee,
Sprouting like daisies that just want to be free.

With wacky roots tickling all of the ground,
They pop out like popcorn, spinning around.
Some wear bow ties, others dance in a trance,
While others just sit back, totally by chance.

Each flower that blooms has a story to tell,
Of pixie dust parties, oh, don't you know well?
The buzz of creation fills up the breeze,
As creatures of whimsy all dance with such ease.

These tiny thoughts grow, like giants in pairs,
Swaying with wonder, no worries or cares.
Seeds of imagination, let's plant them today,
Watch laughs flourish forth in their whimsical play!

Soaring Spirits

Spirits like kites soar high in the sky,
Taking the plunge, oh, my, oh my!
With tails made of laughter and caps made of fun,
They twist and they twirl, in the bright golden sun.

Dancing like dervishes in wild celebration,
They invite everyone to join in the sensation.
A parade of giggles, they float in a line,
With candyfloss dreams, oh, isn't it divine?

Some loop-de-loop while others just glide,
On balloons made of giggles, they take a wild ride.
With wonky little grins and mischief in sight,
They soar through the clouds, a whimsical flight.

As the stars winkle down with a twinkling cheer,
Soaring spirits unite, spreading joy far and near.
With laughter as their fuel, they travel in style,
Soaring high with delight, so stay for a while!

www.ingramcontent.com/pod-product-compliance
Lightning Source LLC
Chambersburg PA
CBHW071845160426
43209CB00003B/423